BEI GRIN MACHT SICH IHR WISSEN BEZAHLT

- Wir veröffentlichen Ihre Hausarbeit, Bachelor- und Masterarbeit

- Ihr eigenes eBook und Buch - weltweit in allen wichtigen Shops

- Verdienen Sie an jedem Verkauf

Jetzt bei www.GRIN.com hochladen und kostenlos publizieren

Bibliografische Information der Deutschen Nationalbibliothek:

Die Deutsche Bibliothek verzeichnet diese Publikation in der Deutschen Nationalbibliografie; detaillierte bibliografische Daten sind im Internet über http://dnb.d-nb.de/ abrufbar.

Dieses Werk sowie alle darin enthaltenen einzelnen Beiträge und Abbildungen sind urheberrechtlich geschützt. Jede Verwertung, die nicht ausdrücklich vom Urheberrechtsschutz zugelassen ist, bedarf der vorherigen Zustimmung des Verlages. Das gilt insbesondere für Vervielfältigungen, Bearbeitungen, Übersetzungen, Mikroverfilmungen, Auswertungen durch Datenbanken und für die Einspeicherung und Verarbeitung in elektronische Systeme. Alle Rechte, auch die des auszugsweisen Nachdrucks, der fotomechanischen Wiedergabe (einschließlich Mikrokopie) sowie der Auswertung durch Datenbanken oder ähnliche Einrichtungen, vorbehalten.

Impressum:

Copyright © 2015 GRIN Verlag
Druck und Bindung: Books on Demand GmbH, Norderstedt Germany
ISBN: 9783668646346

Dieses Buch bei GRIN:

https://www.grin.com/document/412284

John Dorsch

Locating the Spatial Hypothesis Outside the Cartesian Circle. The Sense of Bodily Ownership and The Capacity to Differentiate Between Oneself and Not Oneself

GRIN Verlag

GRIN - Your knowledge has value

Der GRIN Verlag publiziert seit 1998 wissenschaftliche Arbeiten von Studenten, Hochschullehrern und anderen Akademikern als eBook und gedrucktes Buch. Die Verlagswebsite www.grin.com ist die ideale Plattform zur Veröffentlichung von Hausarbeiten, Abschlussarbeiten, wissenschaftlichen Aufsätzen, Dissertationen und Fachbüchern.

Besuchen Sie uns im Internet:

http://www.grin.com/

http://www.facebook.com/grincom

http://www.twitter.com/grin_com

Eberdhard-Karls Universität Tübingen
Philosophisches Seminar
Hauptseminar: The Philosophy and Cognitive Science of Embodied Agency
SS 2015
August 31st, 2015

Locating the Spatial Hypothesis Outside the Cartesian Circle
The Sense of Bodily Ownership and The Capacity to Differentiate Between Oneself and Not Oneself

Abstract

The sense of bodily ownership is perhaps the most important aspect to bodily experience. It gives rise to the body's privilege status as the only object we experience as our own, experienced as subject. But despite how basic this sense is, describing what it is and how it works has been anything but straight-forward. The best explanation for the sense of bodily ownership is arguably the Spatial Hypothesis. It claims that the sense of bodily ownership derives from the spatial representation of the body. Although I support this hypothesis, I argue that past attempts at grounding it risk resulting in a Cartesian circle. I propose a solution distinguishing between capacity and content.

John Joseph Dorsch

HF: Philosophie
NF: Internationale Literaturen

1. The Sense of Bodily Ownership and the Spatial Hypothesis

Compared to all other objects of experience, the body has its unique status because of the privileged perspective we have on it. We view the body 'from the inside'; recently, reference to the body's privileged status has been made even without the scare quotes. One aspect to this internal viewpoint is the sense of bodily ownership: we experience our body as our own. Is this sense of ownership over and above the sense of bodily awareness? Is it a product of it? Does the sense of bodily ownership have its own phenomenology, its own raw feel?

I will leave many of these questions aside. Instead of addressing these arguments, I will concentrate on the discussion that seeks to ground the sense of ownership in bodily awareness. More particularly, I'll concentrate on the research that seeks to ground the sense of ownership in the spatial representation of the body. This means, I assume that the sense of ownership is dependent on bodily awareness, that the sense of ownership has a positive status, that it does have its own, albeit implicit, phenomenology.

Before I present the debates concerning how to ground the sense of ownership, I would like to explain what is meant by an *implicit phenomenology* of bodily ownership. At this moment, while I'm typing, I'm not explicitly aware that my hands are *my* hands. Instead, I'm aware of my thoughts, how they might let themselves be expressed in the English language and, in a less explicit sense, the location of the proper keys on the keyboard. Implicitly, I'm aware of the distance between my fingers, the temperature of the room and its air pressure, and a whole host of other data concerning my body and its environment. I don't need to be explicitly aware of bodily ownership in this moment because nothing requires that I make use of it. As analogy, nothing requires that I make use of the sense of ambient temperature. This is because it is a comfortable eighteen degrees Celsius in my office. But should a massive, purple cloud be ushered in by eastern winds, block the sun and pour rain upon my town, I'd suddenly become aware of the temperature and, as a result, I might turn off my fan. In the same vein, if I had a lesion in the right hemisphere of my brain and suffered from asomatognosia, I'd be aware that my right arm belonged to me, while my left arm did not. Thus, it is in this sense that bodily ownership is implicit: the sense of ownership becomes content for conscious only when a deficit is present.[i]

I would like now to give a quick overview of the differing accounts that ground the sense of ownership. I'll end with the Spatial Hypothesis, followed by reasons for why it is arguably the best explanation. We begin with the question, Does bodily sensation give rise to the sense of ownership? In other words, when I feel a pain in my right hand, do I also sense that the pain is located in a body part that belongs to me? If we dismiss this question, or if we claim bodily sensations do not give rise to the sense of ownership, then we leave the discussion. So for present purposes, let's assume that bodily sensation, such as pain, gives rise to the sense of ownership. This assumption requires justification, however. We could argue that the sense of ownership is grounded in a privileged, inward perception—different than introspection—that has special access to the pain in my right hand, but then we'd need to justify the existence of a wholly different form of perception. Alternatively, we could fix the mode of perception and vary the content of perception. This would mean that the mode of perception that has access to bodily sensations is the exact same perception used in everyday perception of objects. The difference between perceiving bodily sensations and external objects is merely the perceptual content. The question arises now, What makes this content sufficient for grounding the sense of ownership? Is the sense of ownership grounded by the descriptive component to the content, e.g. the stabbing sensation of the pain? Or could it be the spatial component of the content, e.g. the assignment of the sensation to my hand?

I'll focus solely on this latter approach to understanding the relationship between bodily awareness and the sense of bodily ownership. This approach, called the Spatial Hypothesis, claims that the spatial component of the content of perception is the source of the sense of bodily ownership, i.e. the sense of bodily ownership is derived from the spatial representation of the body. In other words, imagine you have a sense of pain in your right hand. The Spatial Hypothesis claims that you know that this pain is in *your* right hand because along with the descriptive component of this sensation, such as a stabbing-sort of pain, there is information about the location of the sensation, and this information falls within the boundaries of the body.

There are three reasons for why the Spatial Hypothesis is a good candidate. First, it is supported by the *measures of embodiment*. Second, spatial representations of the body correspond to the *body schema*, opposed to the body image. Lastly, the Spatial Hypothesis integrates *multimodal representations* of the body, opposed to uni-modal representations. All three reasons will be illustrated shortly, but I'm presenting these reasons merely to motivate the reader, not to argue for the hypothesis.

Measures of Embodiment: The sense of embodiment occurs when something is being processed as a body part; embodiment occurs when this process takes place. The sense of embodiment in not binary: it is not the case that either something is processed as a body part or something is not. There are therefore many different categories of embodiment, aptly shown by the three measures of embodiment: spatial, motor, and affective. Not all are relevant for a sense of ownership, however, for only those measures of embodiment that instantiate what is called self-specific embodiment can ground the sense of ownership.

Self-specific embodiment differs from neutral embodiment. Self-specific refers to those measures of embodiment that can only apply to one's own body, while neutral embodiment can apply to experiences concerning other people's bodies. For example, affective measures of embodiment are neutral; they measure reactions to a hazardous situation, such as a threatening hammer. Studies have shown that this kind of embodiment occurs when someone else is being threatened. The sense of ownership can only be grounded in measures of embodiment that are not shared by both oneself and others, as it doesn't make any sense to talk of a sense of ownership of someone else's body part. There is one spatial measure of embodiment that is self-specific, however.

In order to explicate this self-specific measure of embodiment, some further terminology needs to be introduced. All spatial measures are divided into three frames of reference: the bodily frame, the external frame, and the peripersonal frame, and those that fall into the bodily frame necessarily incur the sense of self-specific embodiment.

The bodily frame instantiates embodiment when something is processed by the representation of the body in space as defined by its boundaries and segmentation into body parts —an example would be a prosthetic limb. The objects processed by the bodily frame cannot be neutral; they are guaranteed to be self-specific. Because the Spatial Hypothesis claims that the sense of ownership is grounded in the spatial representation of the body, it is supported by the results found by the measures of embodiment, which hold that only those measures that are processed within the bodily frame can be self-specific. To put that another way, the spatial representation is implied by the bodily frame, the bodily frame instantiates processes that are guaranteed to be self-specific, and only processes guaranteed to be self-specific can ground the sense of ownership.

The Body Schema: We can talk about the body image, or we can talk about the body schema. The body image is long-term configuration of the body, including more general and psychological aspects, such as how we feel about our body. One's body image is constituted in part by the depositional stance one takes towards one's body. For example, if I believed I'd needed to lose weight in order to look good in a bathing suit, then this belief would integrate into my body image. The body schema, however, is constituted by the sensori-motor functions of the body, i.e. the body schema is composed of the data concerning those physiological components of the body necessary for behavior and action. The body schema is essential in explaining how a subject, suffering from pathological cases of disembodiment, reacquires a sense of embodiment and a sense of bodily ownership. When asking which of the two the Spatial Hypothesis corresponds to, it becomes clear that it corresponds to the body schema due to its integration of sensori-motor information. The link between the Spatial Hypothesis, the body schema, and the sense of bodily ownership supports the claim that the sense of bodily ownership is grounded in the spatial representation of the body.

Multimodal Representations of the Body: Representations of one's own body cannot be accounted for by mere somatosensory representation—visual information is also essential. De Vignemont[1] stresses this by referring to experiments showing visual information increasing the spatial sensitivity of judgments of tactile orientation (Kennent *et al*, 2002). There are also experiments showing how congenitally blind people do not suffer from disorientation linking tactile to visual processing, (Röder *et al*, 2004). Finally, De Vignemont points to studies that show how the representation of bodily boundaries is a combination of kinaesthetic, vestibular, proprioceptive, and tactile sources (Lackner, 1988). This supports the view that the sense of ownership can be manipulated by visual information—something which the rubber hand illusion also shows (Welch and Warren, 1986). That the sense of ownership is constituted not merely by somatosensory representation, but also visual, supports the hypothesis that the sense of ownership derives from the spatial representation of the body.

In the rubber hand illusion, the subject sits at a table, places his left hand on it, and places his right hand under it, so that he cannot see his own right hand. In place of the subject's right hand, a rubber hand now occupies his visual field. The illusion is brought about in the following way: while the rubber hand is brushed, the subject's concealed hand is also brushed. The result is that the subject reports feeling the sensation in the rubber hand, that the rubber hand is even his own hand. What this illusion tells us is that the sense of bodily ownership is constituted also by visual information. These finding pose no problem for the Spatial Hypothesis.

De Vignemont makes this explicit when he says, "The sense of ownership results from the localization of the tactile property within a bodily representation constructed on the basis of information that is available to the subject (e.g. vision, touch and proprioception for most of the people). In the rubber hand illusion, the descriptive component of the tactile sensation is accurate, but not the spatial component."[2]–hence the illusion. De Vignemont continues, "This interpretation is consistent with the spatial hypothesis."[3]

2. Martin's Grounding of the Sense of Bodily Ownership in the Spatial Hypothesis

I'll now explicate Martin's argument for grounding the sense of ownership in the spatial representation of the body. By grounding the sense of ownership in the spatial representation of the body, the privileged role that the body has, its being experienced as one's own, is secured in the experience of the body. More relevant to our present discussion, Martin grounds the sense of ownership in a foundation, where from the sense of ownership can be derived, and this basis

---

1   Frederique De Vignemont. Embodiment, ownership and disownership. Consciousness and Cognition, Elsevier, 2010, pp.1-12.
2   Frederique De Vignemont. Habeas Corpus: The Sense of Ownership of One's Own Body. Mind and Language, Wiley-Blackwell, 2007, p. 438.
3   Ibidem.

corresponds to empirical research and holds up against philosophical arguments.

In elucidating the phenomenological characteristic of the sense of ownership, which he calls "the quality that the body part appears to be part of one's body"[4] Martin makes use of the perceptual account of bodily sensations, i.e. to sense pain is to perceive pain. The difference between perceiving an external object, such as a table, and an internal sensation, such as a pain, is that one's attention has shifted from objects lying outside one's boundaries to "what is going on at or beneath [the] bodily boundary."[5] Thus his conjecture is, "for me to feel as if some part of my body occupies a region of space through having a bodily sensation is for it to seem to me as if that region falls within one of the boundaries of my body."[6] He continues, "The sense one has of the location of sensation brings with it the sense that the location in question falls within one of one's apparent boundaries."[7] Therefore, we can abstract from Martin's reasoning that there are three distinct 'senses' to be distinguished in grounding the sense of bodily ownership: *the sense of location*, *the sense of falling within one's boundaries*, and *the sense of ownership* itself—where the former grounds the latter respectively.

Martin explains this causal chain by providing an example of kinaesthetic experience. When I lift my hands over my head, I'm aware of the position of my hands in space relative to each other. This awareness of the relative position of the hands is "an awareness of the region of space in which my hands are displaced, across a region of space beyond the space in which my body is located, and in which I have neither kinaesthetic nor sensational awareness."[8] Therefore, what I have called generally 'the sense of location' is referred to this passage as 'the awareness of the relative of position of my hands'; but this awareness is not only relative to the different body part, it is also relative to the surrounding space: "[the space] in which I have neither kinaesthetic nor sensational awareness", i.e. the space not occupied by the body.

Martin goes on to say, "the sense of falling within a boundary may be no more than the sense that the location in question is within a space that seems to extend into regions that one could not currently be aware of in this way." By 'this way' he means, self-specific. Therefore, by Martin's own admission, the sense of location is compositional. This sense of location is composed of the self-specific awareness, corresponding to what I sense in this, here, kinaesthetic way, and some other awareness, such as visual, corresponding to some other space that cannot be sensed in the former, kinaesthetic way.

I argue therefore that the sense of falling into one's boundaries is composed by two senses that are not explicit in Martin's reasoning—not merely a sense of location. The two senses

---

4   Martin, M.G.F. Bodily Awareness: A Sense of Ownership. The Body and The Self, MIT Press, Cambridge, 1995, p. 269.
5   Ibid, p.270.
6   Ibidem.
7   Ibid, p.271.
8   Ibidem.

composing the sense of falling within one's boundaries are 1) the sense of a space that is experienced as self-specific and 2) the sense of space that cannot be experienced in a self-specific way. In order to easily reference these two spaces, I'll introduce the terms *ipse* and *alius*. Ipse space refers to that space that is sensed as a location that one can be aware of in some self-specific way. Alius space refers to that space that is sensed as a location in which a) the ipse space is situated and b) that is not sensed as ipse space is sensed.

For example, consider the multimodal aspect to the sense of ownership. Aware of the sense of a pain's location, I'm aware of the space in which the pain is felt and the space surrounding the location of pain; this latter space is not felt and cannot be felt in the same way as the space in which the pain is felt, and these two spaces, ipse and alius, ground the sense of falling within one's boundaries—all of this is inline with Martin's reasoning. Multimodal bodily representation allows for distinct bodily senses to represent the sense of ownership. Some modalities pertain to the experiential content concerning the body, while other modalities pertain to experiential content concerning something other than the body. Both, however, are used in composing the perceptual content that causes the sense of ownership. In determining whether some sensation belongs to oneself, the distinction between the content of ipse and alius space is necessary.

In Martin's argument, the sense of falling within one's boundaries grounds the sense of bodily ownership. I have argued that the sense of falling within one's boundaries is dependent on two senses: the sense of an ipse space and the sense of an alius space. By Martin's own account, distinguishing between ipse space and alius space creates the boundaries that separate bodily sensations from sensations belonging to the world of other things. Therefore, Martin's reasoning rests on one of two possibilities: either his reasoning rests on the difference between the *content* of these two spaces—I'll call this the content option—or it rests on the *capacity* to differentiate between the two spaces—I'll call the capacity option.

If the difference between the *content* of ipse and alius space is assumed by the sense of falling within one's boundaries, then the sense of ownership rests on the difference between oneself and not oneself. This is a Cartesian circle because the difference in content between oneself and not oneself ought to be proved by the the sense of falling within one's boundaries.

For example, when examining the content option, we have at the outset two different contents, each belonging to a different sense datum. The first is a sense datum of a hand touching an apple. The second is the sense datum of an apple (being touched). The content option claims that the difference in sensuous content is used to ground the sense that the first datum falls within one's bodily boundaries, and this sense is used to ground the sense that the first datum belongs to oneself. I argue that the content option assumes the sense of bodily ownership and therefore presents us with a Cartesian circle; this is because the sense datum of the hand is felt as occupying a space that is experienced in a self-specific way, and this sense datum is distributed across a space that is felt as experienced in a non-self-specific way, therefore what is my body and what is not my body is assumed at the outset, i.e. self-specificity is used to start and terminate the casual chain.

If, however, the *capacity* to differentiate between ipse space and alius space is assumed, then the the sense of ownership rests on a cognitive faculty efficaciously equipped to organize perceptual content into ipse and alius spaces. For example, I see and touch a Braeburn apple. It is firm and has a red-orange vertical streaky appearance. Along with this sense datum of the hand touching the apple, and the datum of the smooth and firm sensation of the apple itself, is the datum concerning the location of these data. Before it is determined whether one datum falls within my bodily boundaries, two constraints need to be applied. These constraints impinge upon the sensory modalities, differentiating the ipse space from the alius space, and once the data is checked against these constraints, I have a sense of the content of the ipse space and the content of the alius space. Now I can distinguish between the apple that I'm feeling and the hand that feels the apple. And as a result, that which turns out to be the content of the ipse space, my hand, is felt as *my* hand. With the capacity option, what is presupposed is not the content of ipse and alius space, but the capacity to differentiate between the perceptual content of these contrasting spaces.

Does not the capacity to differentiate depend on the some notion of what makes the datum different from one another? In other words, how does one know how to distinguish between two things, when knowledge of the difference between the two is assumed at the outset? For example, I'd need to already have some concept of good writing to know how to distinguish good from bad writing, but how can I have some concept of good writing without having already distinguished the good from the bad writing? So presented, it would seem that the capacity option is the chicken, while the content option is the egg.

Concerning distinguishing between sensations that fall into ipse space from those that falls into alius space, however, it might be possible to talk about hard-wired, biological 'knowledge'. Were that so, we could claim that evolution has equipped the nervous system with the capacity to differentiate between the two spaces; meaning, along with this capacity, there are certain prescribed rules for determining whether a sense datum belongs to ipse or to alius space. These prescribed rules might well be the hard work of Darwinian evolution. If this claim is tenable, then we have wiggled our way out of another vicious circle.

i Thus the sense of bodily ownership has the property Heidegger refered to as "inconspiciuous intimacy"; meaning, this sense only becomes apparent in "the deficient modes of concern.", ie when a de-ficit is present, imploring us to act. "*Die vorgängige Zuhandenheit der jeweiligen Gegend hat in einem noch ursprüglicheren Sinne als das Sein des Zuhanden den /Charakter der unauffälligen Vertrautheit/. Sie wird selbst nur sichtbar in der Weise des Auffallens bei einem umsichtigen Entdecken des Zuhandenen und zwar in den deizienten Modi des Besorgens.*" (Heidegger, P.104)

Bibliography

Frederique De Vignemont. Habeas Corpus: The Sense of Ownership of One's Own Body. Mind and Language, Wiley-Blackwell, 2007, pp.427-449.

Frederique De Vignemont. Embodiment, ownership and disownership. Consciousness and Cognition, Elsevier, 2010, pp.1-12.

Heidegger, Martin. Sein und Zeit. Max Niemeyer Verlag, Tübingen, 2006.

Martin, M.G.F. Bodily Awareness: A Sense of Ownership. The Body and The Self, MIT Press, Cambridge, 1995, pp. 267-290.

BEI GRIN MACHT SICH IHR WISSEN BEZAHLT

- Wir veröffentlichen Ihre Hausarbeit, Bachelor- und Masterarbeit

- Ihr eigenes eBook und Buch - weltweit in allen wichtigen Shops

- Verdienen Sie an jedem Verkauf

Jetzt bei www.GRIN.com hochladen und kostenlos publizieren